Table of Contents

So, You Want An Answer From God

Richard King, Sr

OutFlow

Publishing

Valdese, North Carolina

So, You Want An Answer From God
Second Edition
Copyright © 2019 by Richard King, Sr.

Edited by Allen King
Published by OutFlow Publishing
Valdese, North Carolina 28690
www.outflowpublishing.com

ISBN-13: 978-1-7329995-1-0

Printed in the United States of America.

All scripture reference are from the King James Version
unless otherwise noted.
KING JAMES VERSION (KJV): KING JAMES VERSION,
public domain.

Preface

So, You Want An Answer From God

You, or perhaps a family member or close friend, are in a totally desperate situation, and so you pray. However, it seems the more you pray, the more desperate the situation becomes. You are sincere in your praying, and in your believing, but it seems that the heavens have become as brass, and your prayers are falling on deaf ears. It is as if God is a million miles away. How does a sincere child of Almighty God go from that point of desperation and confusion, to answered prayer?

People pray and ask God for something. Then, when it doesn't come to pass, and they receive nothing from the Lord, they become filled with all kinds of emotions.

They get discouraged. They get frustrated. Many even become angry with God. So, what does it take to get an answer to your prayer in a time of urgent need?

1

A Sanctified Life Empowers Prayer

In the biblical days, the people had to sanctify themselves. They had to become the holy people that God intended them to be. If they wanted something from God, they had to become Godly. They had to become a holy, set apart people. This has always been in God's plan for us.

The Christian church of today has become too self-sufficient, and self-reliant. Christians today do not seem to need to call upon God, until there arises that time of desperation--that time when we've come to the end of our own ability. Today, people trust in material goods, in homes, cars, and bank accounts.

In the time of Joshua, the children of Israel had just won a great battle against a powerful enemy. They had conquered the great city of Jericho. The sixth chapter of the Book of Joshua tells the story.

Joshua 6:16 And it came to pass at the seventh time, when the priests blew with the trumpets, Joshua said unto the people, Shout; for the LORD hath given you the city.

17 And the city shall be accursed, even it, and all that are therein, to the LORD: only Rahab the harlot shall live, she and all that are with her in the house, because she hid the messengers that we sent.

18 And ye, in any wise keep yourselves from the accursed thing, lest ye make yourselves accursed, when ye take of the accursed thing, and make the camp of Israel a curse, and trouble it.

19 But all the silver, and gold, and vessels of brass and iron, are consecrated unto the LORD: they shall come into the treasury of the LORD.

20 So the people shouted when the priests blew with the trumpets: and it came to pass, when the people heard the sound of the trumpet, and the people shouted with a great shout, that the wall fell down flat, so that the people went up into the city, every man straight before him, and they took the city.

21 And they utterly destroyed all that was in the city, both man and woman, young and old, and ox, and sheep, and ass, with the edge of the sword.

22 But Joshua had said unto the two men that had spied out the country, Go into the harlot's house, and bring out thence the woman, and all that she hath, as ye sware unto her.

23 And the young men that were spies went in, and brought out Rahab, and her father, and her mother, and her brethren, and all that she had; and they brought out all her kindred, and left them without the camp of Israel.

24 And they burnt the city with fire, and all that was therein: only the silver, and the gold, and the vessels of brass and of iron, they put into the treasury of the house of the LORD.

25 And Joshua saved Rahab the harlot alive, and her father's household, and all that she had; and she dwelleth in Israel even unto this day; because she hid the messengers, which Joshua sent to spy out Jericho.

26 And Joshua adjured them at that time, saying, Cursed be the man before the LORD, that riseth up and buildeth this city Jericho: he shall lay the foundation thereof in his firstborn, and in his youngest son shall he set up the gates of it.

27 So the LORD was with Joshua; and his fame was noised throughout all the country. - Joshua 6:16-27

However, in the very next chapter we read,

Joshua 7:1 But the children of Israel committed a trespass in the accursed thing: for Achan, the son of Carmi, the son of Zabdi, the son of Zerah, of the tribe of Judah, took of the accursed thing: and the anger of the LORD was kindled against the children of Israel.

2 And Joshua sent men from Jericho to Ai, which is beside Bethaven, on the east side of Bethel, and spake unto them, saying, Go up and view the country. And the men went up and viewed Ai.

3 And they returned to Joshua, and said unto him, Let not all the people go up; but let about two or three thousand men go up and smite Ai; and make not all the people to labour thither; for they are but few.

4 So there went up thither of the people about three thousand men: and they fled before the men of Ai.

5 And the men of Ai smote of them about thirty and six men: for they chased them from before the gate even unto Shebarim, and smote them in the going down: wherefore the hearts of the people melted, and became as water.

God will never bless when there is sin in the camp. The Israelites had just conquered mighty Jericho. Now, little Ai defeats the mighty army of Joshua. You can never afford to leave God out of the mix.

Every step toward Jericho was led by the Lord. Jericho was a desperate situation. If Israel was to make it to the promised land, they had to defeat Jericho. They placed their complete trust in God and listened to the instruction which God gave to Joshua. Then, they were responsible to obey those instructions.

They had to march around the city the right number of times; they had to shout and blow the trumpets at the right time. The survival of Israel depended on doing things exactly as God had instructed.

Ai was insignificant. So, the Israelite army approached it on their own, leaving God completely out of the plan.

Then, there is an element of sin in the camp. Achan had disobeyed God and had taken what God had said to leave alone because it was cursed.

If you are to receive anything from God, you must get to the point of putting God first.

Joshua 7:6 And Joshua rent his clothes, and fell to the earth upon his face before the ark of the LORD until the eventide, he and the elders of Israel, and put dust upon their heads.

7 And Joshua said, Alas, O Lord GOD, wherefore hast thou at all brought this people over Jordan, to deliver us into the hand of the Amorites, to destroy us? would to God we had been content, and dwelt on the other side Jordan!

8 O Lord, what shall I say, when Israel turneth their backs before their enemies!

9 For the Canaanites and all the inhabitants of the land shall hear of it, and shall environ us round, and cut off our name from the earth: and what wilt thou do unto thy great name?

10 And the LORD said unto Joshua, Get thee up; wherefore liest thou thus upon thy face?

11 Israel hath sinned, and they have also transgressed my covenant which I commanded them: for they have even taken of the accursed thing, and have also stolen, and dissembled also, and they have put it even among their own stuff.

12 Therefore the children of Israel could not stand before their enemies, but turned their backs before their enemies, because they were accursed: neither will I be with you any more, except ye destroy the accursed from among you.

13 Up, sanctify the people, and say, Sanctify yourselves against tomorrow: for thus saith the LORD God of Israel, There is an accursed thing in the midst of thee, O Israel: thou canst not stand before thine enemies, until ye take away the accursed thing from among you.

14 In the morning therefore ye shall be brought according to your tribes: and it

shall be, that the tribe which the LORD taketh shall come according to the families thereof; and the family which the LORD shall take shall come by households; and the household which the LORD shall take shall come man by man.

15 And it shall be, that he that is taken with the accursed thing shall be burnt with fire, he and all that he hath: because he hath transgressed the covenant of the LORD, and because he hath wrought folly in Israel.

God told Joshua to get up off his face and sanctify the people. Today's church has seemingly lost this vital part of the Christian walk. That part of coming out from among the sins of the world, and separating ourselves to the kingdom work of God. If a Christian forgets who they are in the Lord and they begin to compromise with the world they will never develop a prayer life that will get them through the desperate times in their lives; and desperate times come to us all.

I have observed this in the church where I have been the senior pastor for over twenty-five years now. Christians sit in church like nothing is going on, service after service, having no spiritual growth in their lives. Getting them involved in the work of the church seems to be an impossible task. Then, some tragic situation comes to them or a close family member, and all of a sudden they show up at the altar, weeping before the

Lord, with a weak prayer life. Yet, they expect God to send them a miracle. It simply does not work that way in the Kingdom of Almighty God.

Even when we are doing things in a way that seems to be the right way, are we following God's way? ***"There is a way that seemeth right unto a man, but the end thereof are the ways of death"*** (Proverbs 16:25). God has a way, and His way is not man's way. God is never slack in His promise.

There was the time when King David was making plans to bring the ark of the covenant back to Jerusalem. In 1 Chronicles chapter 13, the people of Israel attempted to bring the ark home on a new cart, which was never the way God planned to carry the ark. Finally, in chapter 15, they decide to do it God's way.

> **1 Chronicles 15:1 And David made him houses in the city of David, and prepared a place for the ark of God, and pitched for it a tent.**
>
> **2 Then David said, None ought to carry the ark of God but the Levites: for them hath the LORD chosen to carry the ark of God, and to minister unto him for ever.**
>
> **3 And David gathered all Israel together to Jerusalem, to bring up the ark of the LORD unto his place, which he had prepared for it.**

4 And David assembled the children of Aaron, and the Levites:

5 Of the sons of Kohath; Uriel the chief, and his brethren an hundred and twenty:

6 Of the sons of Merari; Asaiah the chief, and his brethren two hundred and twenty:

7 Of the sons of Gershom; Joel the chief, and his brethren an hundred and thirty:

8 Of the sons of Elizaphan; Shemaiah the chief, and his brethren two hundred:

9 Of the sons of Hebron; Eliel the chief, and his brethren fourscore:

10 Of the sons of Uzziel; Amminadab the chief, and his brethren an hundred and twelve.

11 And David called for Zadok and Abiathar the priests, and for the Levites, for Uriel, Asaiah, and Joel, Shemaiah, and Eliel, and Amminadab,

12 And said unto them, Ye are the chief of the fathers of the Levites: sanctify yourselves, both ye and your brethren, that ye may bring up the ark of the LORD God of Israel unto the place that I have prepared for it.

13 For because ye did it not at the first, the LORD our God made a breach upon us, for that we sought him not after the due order.

14 So the priests and the Levites sanctified themselves to bring up the ark of the LORD God of Israel.

15 And the children of the Levites bare the ark of God upon their shoulders with the staves thereon, as Moses commanded according to the word of the LORD.

After David had called together the priests to carry the Ark of God, he told them to sanctify themselves for the task at hand. Each time there was a war to be won, or a great task to be carried out, the people were instructed to sanctify themselves before they were to go forth.

2

Dedication to Prayer

I believe there are times when God wants to do great things for and through us, but our lack of faith and our lack of dedication hinder us from receiving what God has to offer us. God wants us to be prepared by fully surrendering ourselves to His divine will. If you want to win a war, surrender it completely to God. If you want God's blessings on your family, surrender it completely to God, If you need God to show up in a desperate time, sanctify yourself, and give it to God.

"Now I lay me down to sleep" prayers simply will not get things done in the Kingdom of God. It takes total surrender. It is total surrender, not just commitment, that removes doubt and fear. We fail too many times in our commitment, but when we surrender, we become the servant of God.

James tells us,

> *James 1:2 My brethren, count it all joy when ye fall into divers temptations;*
>
> *3 Knowing this, that the trying of your faith worketh patience.*
>
> *4 But let patience have her perfect work, that ye may be perfect and entire, wanting nothing.*
>
> *5 If any of you lack wisdom, let him ask of God, that giveth to all men liberally, and upbraideth not; and it shall be given him.*
>
> *6 But let him ask in faith, nothing wavering. For he that wavereth is like a wave of the sea driven with the wind and tossed.*
>
> *7 For let not that man think that he shall receive any thing of the Lord.*
>
> *8 A double minded man is unstable in all his ways.*

Jesus rebuked His disciples on several occasions for their lack of faith.

James further instructs us on how we ought to live if we want an answer to our prayers, especially when there is a desperate need.

> *James 4:1 From whence come wars and fightings among you? come they not hence, even of your lusts that war in your members?*
>
> *2 Ye lust, and have not: ye kill, and desire to have, and cannot obtain: ye fight and war, yet ye have not, because ye ask not.*
>
> *3 Ye ask, and receive not, because ye ask amiss, that ye may consume it upon your lusts.*
>
> *4 Ye adulterers and adulteresses, know ye not that the friendship of the world is enmity with God? whosoever therefore will be a friend of the world is the enemy of God.*
>
> *5 Do ye think that the scripture saith in vain, The spirit that dwelleth in us lusteth to envy?*
>
> *6 But he giveth more grace. Wherefore he saith, God resisteth the proud, but giveth grace unto the humble.*
>
> *7 Submit yourselves therefore to God. Resist the devil, and he will flee from you.*

8 Draw nigh to God, and he will draw nigh to you. Cleanse your hands, ye sinners; and purify your hearts, ye double minded.

9 Be afflicted, and mourn, and weep: let your laughter be turned to mourning, and your joy to heaviness.

10 Humble yourselves in the sight of the Lord, and he shall lift you up.

11 Speak not evil one of another, brethren. He that speaketh evil of his brother, and judgeth his brother, speaketh evil of the law, and judgeth the law: but if thou judge the law, thou art not a doer of the law, but a judge.

12 There is one lawgiver, who is able to save and to destroy: who art thou that judgest another?

13 Go to now, ye that say, To day or to morrow we will go into such a city, and continue there a year, and buy and sell, and get gain:

14 Whereas ye know not what shall be on the morrow. For what is your life? It is even a vapour, that appeareth for a little time, and then vanisheth away.

15 For that ye ought to say, If the Lord will, we shall live, and do this, or that.

16 But now ye rejoice in your boastings: all such rejoicing is evil.

17 Therefore to him that knoweth to do good, and doeth it not, to him it is sin.

When a Christian begins to live James chapter 4, they should have no problem getting their prayers answered. Especially verse 7 and 8, **"Submit yourselves therefore to God. Resist the devil, and he will flee from you. 8 Draw nigh to God, and he will draw nigh to you. Cleanse your hands, ye sinners; and purify your hearts, ye double minded."**

Then some would say, "Well I'm not a sinner." The word sinner used here means, "To miss the mark and so not share in the prize. Your faults, your offense, your trespasses." It goes back to verse 17, *"Therefore to him that knoweth to do good, and doeth it not, to him it is sin."* It's those sins of omission.

We have no problem when the cliché prayers are not answered. We have no problem not getting an answer to the pharisee type prayers, or the repetitive prayers we pray every time we want to talk to God.

However, when a tragedy strikes home everything changes. When the doctor uses the word "cancer", or you get the pink slip at work saying you no longer have employment here, and you know this could cost you everything you have worked for all your life. It is in those times when you get a phone call telling you that your child is in the hospital and may die from an overdose of drugs. These are the times when you really need to get in touch with your Heavenly Father because now, He is the only One who can help you.

Now, you begin to think about all the times you should have stayed close to the Lord. You think about the many times you could have gone to church and could have been faithful to the things of God's kingdom work, and you stubbornly stayed home, or went elsewhere to have family fun on the Lord's day. You think about all those times you did these things, and you realize you were teaching your children that God and His Church were not that important.

Now, you wonder if God will even listen if you pray. I assure you that He will. God loves us even in our worst of times, and He really does care about our problems and He desires to be our ever present help in your times of need. God loved us even when we were sinners.

In order to receive anything from God, you must first get serious, and seriously sanctified, seriously focused on the things of God. Your house must be set in order. You must put aside everything that will hinder you in any way, shape, or form.

3

Our Part in The Process

The twelfth chapter of the Book of Hebrews offers some great instruction on what it takes to receive an answer to prayer in a drastic situation.

> **Hebrews 12:1 Wherefore seeing we also are compassed about with so great a cloud of witnesses, let us lay aside every weight, and the sin which doth so easily beset us, and let us run with patience the race that is set before us,**
>
> **2 Looking unto Jesus the author and finisher of our faith; who for the joy that was set before him endured the cross,**

despising the shame, and is set down at the right hand of the throne of God.

3 For consider him that endured such contradiction of sinners against himself, lest ye be wearied and faint in your minds.

4 Ye have not yet resisted unto blood, striving against sin.

5 And ye have forgotten the exhortation which speaketh unto you as unto children, My son, despise not thou the chastening of the Lord, nor faint when thou art rebuked of him:

6 For whom the Lord loveth he chasteneth, and scourgeth every son whom he receiveth.

7 If ye endure chastening, God dealeth with you as with sons; for what son is he whom the father chasteneth not?

8 But if ye be without chastisement, whereof all are partakers, then are ye bastards, and not sons.

9 Furthermore we have had fathers of our flesh which corrected us, and we gave them reverence: shall we not much rather be in subjection unto the Father of spirits, and live?

10 For they verily for a few days chastened us after their own pleasure; but he for our profit, that we might be partakers of his holiness.

11 Now no chastening for the present seemeth to be joyous, but grievous: nevertheless afterward it yieldeth the peaceable fruit of righteousness unto them which are exercised thereby.

12 Wherefore lift up the hands which hang down, and the feeble knees;

13 And make straight paths for your feet, lest that which is lame be turned out of the way; but let it rather be healed.

14 Follow peace with all men, and holiness, (Sanctification,) without which no man shall see the Lord:

15 Looking diligently lest any man fail, (Fall from,) of the grace of God; lest any root of bitterness springing up trouble you, and thereby many be defiled;

First, you need to realize the greatest problem with unanswered prayer is the person who is praying. It is always easy to place the blame on someone else. There must first be a change in lifestyle.

It is like a person who has lived a pretty good life. They have gone to church and have tried to live as good for the Lord as they thought they could. Then, they come down to the end of their life. They look back and ponder things that they have done wrong, and the things they should have done that they failed to do.

They realize the only hope they now have to escape the fires of hell is to set their house in order as King Hezekiah did, in **Isaiah 38:1 "In those days was Hezekiah sick unto death. And the prophet Isaiah the son of Amoz came to him, and said unto him, 'Thus saith the LORD, Set thine house in order; for thou shalt die, and not live.'"**

We know that Hezekiah turned his face to the wall and prayed and God gave him 15 more years. If he had accepted the fact that he was destined to die it would have meant his death. When he got serious with God, God got serious with him and he lived.

For much too long, Christians have taken prayer for granted, and in doing so we have taken God for granted as well. Answered prayer comes through realizing God is simply waiting on us to get our self in line with the revealed truth of the Word of God.

Serving God is the most serious thing a person can do in life. Serving God has never been for wimps or cowards. Anyone can serve the devil. It takes very little effort to be a sinner. It takes a real man or woman to be a biblical Christian, that is to be truly Christ-like.

When you come up against desperation in life, and you realize God is the only answer, you cannot afford to waste your prayer effort on a simple, one time prayer.

You are desperate, you need and must have an answer. You can have what you need from God when you get as serious as your problem. You must get as serious as Hezekiah.

The old time preachers used to call people who couldn't dedicate themselves totally to God, fence-straddlers. They were considered to be on God's side while everything was going their way, and serving the devil when things went against them. Those who straddle the fence will never get God's attention, and will never get an answer to a desperate prayer. Many good people die from disease because of this.

It's always easier to plow around a stump than to remove it, when you're preparing a new ground for planting a crop. People of God live so far below what their Heavenly Father has planned for their lives.

One of the saddest scenarios that I can imagine would be for a child of God to one day stand before our Lord, and to then realize all that we could have done, and all that we might have become in Christ. If we could only realize the riches of His glory, and what power we truly possess. What opportunities are we allowing to slip away because we refuse to see God in every one of our circumstances?

I do not want to realize too late the problems that I could have flown over with eagles' wings, rather than dragging my feet through them. I don't want to live life in discouragement, distress, disappointment, and defeat, when I have been promised joy that is "unspeakable and full of glory."

There is so much available to us, as children of God. However, in order to receive, we have to learn what it means to really trust God.

I had to learn that myself. A few months ago, I faced a desperate time in a family situation.

My Grandson went to college to study Police Science and was hired as a police officer in the city where he lived. During his rookie period, he had an accident in his police car and was asked to resign, because he was a rookie officer. He was doing a great job, but it was the rules and he lost his first job. He was then hired by another department and worked there for over six years. The police chief of the town moved on to become the Mayor and another officer took his place; this new chief disliked my grandson and after his long tenure on the job he was again forced to resign, because of a vindictive spirit of the new police chief. The only job he could now get was a Special Police position with a security firm. While working there and playing with his band on the side, he was doing okay financially but was never satisfied with the job. He left his band and repented of his sins and became a part of our church; playing his guitar in the church band and living a good Christian life.

He met a young lady who attended the church and they were married. His wife already had a three year old daughter before they were married, and later they had a beautiful new daughter and a lot more responsibility. He had applied for positions with several different police departments because he wanted to do what he called "regular Police work". Because of the vindictive spirit of his old police chief, he was turned down, and could not get a position with any department. He became so discouraged that he was about to give up on Police work all together.

I began to pray every day and night about his situation. Then one day I realized that I was praying in the wrong way. Nothing had changed. I was doing all the talking and not allowing God to speak.

I am the lead pastor of a great church, and I should know how to pray. I'm not a novice. I have been at this a long time. I thought I had it all together, but I received God's rebuke.

God let me know that I had no idea, when it comes to praying for an answer in a desperate situation. So, my first priority became asking God how to approach this situation biblically in order to be pleasing to Him. As I began to search for the divine will of God, I learned a lot through a search of the scriptures on how to receive an answer from God in desperate situations.

We always go to what Jesus said in the Gospels.

John 14:13 And whatsoever ye shall ask in my name, that will I do, that the Father may be glorified in the Son.

14 If ye shall ask any thing in my name, I will do it.

There was a time we read of, in Matthew 17, when the disciples could not cast a devil out of a man's son. Jesus responded, in verse 20, "**Because of your unbelief: for verily I say unto you, If ye have faith as a grain of mustard seed, ye shall say unto this mountain, Remove hence to yonder place; and it shall remove; and nothing shall be impossible unto you.**"

Jesus also declared, in **Mark 16:17 "And these signs shall follow them that believe; In my name shall they cast out devils; they shall speak with new tongues; 18 They shall take up serpents; and if they drink any deadly thing, it shall not hurt them; they shall lay hands on the sick, and they shall recover."**

We have all these promises in the Word of God, and we know they are true sayings of our Lord. but we take them out of context, and think they give us unmerited favor with God, just because we are Christians. I found in my time of desperation that this is not the case at all. If we want answered prayers, we must set our lives in order with the word of God.

Some things are only done through prayer and fasting. I began to fast and pray and seek the guidance of my Heavenly Father. I had to examine my own life.

My Grandson had received rejection letters from every Police Department to which he had applied. This became very discouraging to the entire family. His career in police work seemed to be at an end. He was totally ready to give up. He was told things like, "When you get to the end of your rope, tie a knot and hold on." This is good in theory, but not reality when you've lost hope. He had done his part, had finished his college work, and had worked in his field of expertise. Yet, he was forced by a vindictive police chief to resign. Now, he could not even get anyone to give him a chance. When his record would get checked the vindictive red flag was always there, and no one would overlook it.

It came to the point that God was his only hope, and his confidence was shattered. He had prayed and felt that God didn't owe him anything because of his life style in rock music, before coming back to church and renewing his commitment to the Lord.

The devil always wants us to believe this kind of lie so he can keep us in bondage. This is why the prophesy of the coming of Jesus as Lord in Isaiah 53 is so very important.

> **Isaiah 53:1 Who hath believed our report? and to whom is the arm of the LORD revealed?**
>
> **2 For he shall grow up before him as a tender plant, and as a root out of a dry ground: he hath no form nor comeliness; and when we shall see him, there is no beauty that we should desire him.**

3 He is despised and rejected of men; a man of sorrows, and acquainted with grief: and we hid as it were our faces from him; he was despised, and we esteemed him not.

4 Surely he hath borne our griefs, and carried our sorrows: yet we did esteem him stricken, smitten of God, and afflicted.

5 But he was wounded for our transgressions, he was bruised for our iniquities: the chastisement of our peace was upon him; and with his stripes we are healed.

6 All we like sheep have gone astray; we have turned every one to his own way; and the LORD hath laid on him the iniquity of us all.

7 He was oppressed, and he was afflicted, yet he opened not his mouth: he is brought as a lamb to the slaughter, and as a sheep before her shearers is dumb, so he openeth not his mouth.

8 He was taken from prison and from judgment: and who shall declare his generation? for he was cut off out of the land of the living: for the transgression of my people was he stricken.

9 And he made his grave with the wicked, and with the rich in his death; because he had done no violence, neither was any deceit in his mouth.

10 Yet it pleased the LORD to bruise him; he hath put him to grief: when thou shalt make his soul an offering for sin, he shall see his seed, he shall prolong his days, and the pleasure of the LORD shall prosper in his hand.

11 He shall see of the travail of his soul, and shall be satisfied: by his knowledge shall my righteous servant justify many; for he shall bear their iniquities.

12 Therefore will I divide him a portion with the great, and he shall divide the spoil with the strong; because he hath poured out his soul unto death: and he was numbered with the transgressors; and he bare the sin of many, and made intercession for the transgressors.

Even with all this, there are times when someone must stand in the gap and intercede for the needs of others. Pray **Isaiah 35:3-4** on their behalf: **"Strengthen ye the weak hands, and confirm the feeble knees. 4 Say to them that are of a fearful heart, Be strong, fear not: behold, your God will come with vengeance, even God with a recompense; he will come and save you."**

My grandson attempted to go the police department and review his record, which State Law says he can do, and was denied that privilege. There was no other recourse. Every avenue was closed. There was no hope left, "But God." He was no longer able to pray and believe for himself, therefore it became my lot to stand in the gap for my grandson in his desperate time.

After much seeking after God, whom I had served for many years, I had to rethink everything I had ever known about prayer and intercession. I had to learn to live **Hebrews 12:11-14, "Now no chastening for the present seemeth to be joyous, but grievous: nevertheless afterward it yieldeth the peaceable fruit of righteousness unto them which are exercised thereby. Wherefore lift up the hands which hang down, and the feeble knees; And make straight paths for your feet, lest that which is lame be turned out of the way; but let it rather be healed. Follow peace with all men, and holiness, without which no man shall see the Lord:**

First of all, I had to go to some people and ask for forgiveness and make some things right. I had to pray and ask God for forgiveness for my times of slackness. I had to rethink my entire prayer life.

I learned very quickly that when you make this kind of commitment to God, the devil will become a personal enemy. You learn to fight spiritual battles in a different way.

I lived eight years in the military, learning how to fight battles in the natural sense, but I have learned that spiritual battles are very different. In spiritual battles, we fight an enemy we can't always see with our natural eyes.

One thing I learned was that even those in your own family, and those close to you in church will attempt to discourage you in your fight. My very close family members would say things like, "It doesn't look like he will ever get another job in police work." "Well he just got another rejection letter, looks like he may as well look for another career, police work doesn't seem like its going to work out." My response was, "SHUT UP! don't mess with my faith! God is going to do this, and no one is going to bring doubt into my prayer life. No one is going to hinder my faith. He is going to work again with a good police force, doing what he feels is his calling. Man cannot do it, but I serve a God that can and will do this.

Rejection after rejection came after that, and when they came, I fasted and prayed harder. Even when my grandson seemed to be giving up, I would tell him it was going to happen. God was at work and he was going to hear good news any day. Every time a rejection letter came, the devil would come to my mind trying to bring doubt, and I had to rebuke him, and draw close to my Heavenly Father for comfort and assurance, which always strengthened my faith.

This didn't happen overnight. I had to learn that time doesn't mean anything to God. Sometimes, we are made to wait on things to fall into place, but knowing they WILL fall into place. We are sometimes made to live what Jude wrote. Contend for the faith. Fight for the faith. Defeat the enemy of our faith. It sometimes takes weeks, months, or years. Other times, it only takes days. Sometimes, our miracle comes instantly.

There comes the time when we have to stand on Paul's exhortation to the Ephesians.

> **Ephesians 6:10 Finally, my brethren, be strong in the Lord, and in the power of his might.**
>
> **11 Put on the whole armour of God, that ye may be able to stand against the wiles of the devil.**
>
> **12 For we wrestle not against flesh and blood, but against principalities, against powers, against the rulers of the darkness of this world, against spiritual wickedness in high places.**
>
> **13 Wherefore take unto you the whole armour of God, that ye may be able to withstand in the evil day, and having done all, to stand.**
>
> **14 Stand therefore, having your loins girt about with truth, and having on the breastplate of righteousness;**
>
> **15 And your feet shod with the preparation of the gospel of peace;**

16 Above all, taking the shield of faith, wherewith ye shall be able to quench all the fiery darts of the wicked.

17 And take the helmet of salvation, and the sword of the Spirit, which is the word of God:

18 Praying always with all prayer and supplication in the Spirit, and watching thereunto with all perseverance and supplication for all saints;

Remember, God uses the foolish things of the world to confound the wise. He has his own way to bring an answer to prayers of desperation. He makes a way when there seems to be no way. He can still part the waters and make a highway through the sea of our troubles.

God amazed me with the way He came and brought an answer to my Grandson's desperate hopeless situation. I have a good friend who married his old High School sweetheart. She found out that my grandson wanted to go back into police work and had all those things working against him and was about to give up.

This woman happened to have a relative who was a ranking officer in a great city police department. So, she made a phone call that began the working of a miracle. Through much biblically-based prayer and fasting, my grandson was asked to send an application, which he did with reservations because of his past rejections. This time, everything fell into place, and today he is a police officer in good standing with a great department.

If you need healing, or you have a family member who needs healing from some dreaded disease, remember God is the only hope in your desperate situation. If you are willing to pay the price of sacrificing yourself, and doing it God's way, He will take care of whatever you need.

The Word of God is true when it declares, in **Psalm 34:7-9, "The angel of the LORD encampeth round about them that fear him, and delivereth them. O taste and see that the LORD is good: blessed is the man that trusteth in him. O fear the LORD, ye his saints: for there is no want to them that fear him."**

Learn to embrace scripture passages that feed your faith, such as

> **Psalm 103:1 Bless the Lord, O my soul: and all that is within me, bless his holy name.**
>
> **2 Bless the LORD, O my soul, and forget not all his benefits:**
>
> **3 Who forgiveth all thine iniquities; who healeth all thy diseases;**
>
> **4 Who redeemeth thy life from destruction; who crowneth thee with lovingkindness and tender mercies;**

5 Who satisfieth thy mouth with good things; so that thy youth is renewed like the eagle's.

6 The LORD executeth righteousness and judgment for all that are oppressed.

7 He made known his ways unto Moses, his acts unto the children of Israel.

8 The LORD is merciful and gracious, slow to anger, and plenteous in mercy.

9 He will not always chide: neither will he keep his anger for ever.

10 He hath not dealt with us after our sins; nor rewarded us according to our iniquities.

11 For as the heaven is high above the earth, so great is his mercy toward them that fear him.

12 As far as the east is from the west, so far hath he removed our transgressions from us.

13 Like as a father pitieth his children, so the LORD pitieth them that fear him.

4

Desperation Requires Separation

I have met so many Christians who pray for a miracle with a substandard prayer life and want to blame God for not answering. I had to realize that I'm just a servant of the lord.

When the Lord came to talk to Abraham before the destruction of Sodom, Abraham saw himself as a servant of the Lord, and even referred to himself in that manner. In Malachi 4:4, God considered Moses a Servant.

We say that when we get to Heaven, we want to hear the Lord say, "Well done thy good and faithful servant." However, sometimes we develop the attitude that we are so close to God that He owes us something. If you have this attitude, you will never receive an answer to a desperate prayer.

When I was led of God into preparation for the answer to my desperate prayer for my Grandson, I began to feel demonic powers come against me as never before in my walk with God. God led me to Paul's writings to Timothy.

> **2 Timothy 2:1 Thou therefore, my son, be strong in the grace that is in Christ Jesus.**
>
> **2 And the things that thou hast heard of me among many witnesses, the same commit thou to faithful men, who shall be able to teach others also.**
>
> **3 Thou therefore endure hardness, as a good soldier of Jesus Christ.**
>
> **4 No man that warreth entangleth himself with the affairs of this life; that he may please him who hath chosen him to be a soldier.**
>
> **5 And if a man also strive for masteries, yet is he not crowned, except he strive lawfully.**
>
> **6 The husbandman that laboureth must be first partaker of the fruits.**

**7 Consider what I say; and the Lord give
the understanding in all things.**

I had to realize that I had stepped onto the front line of battle. I realized that God was about to teach me a very powerful truth that I had not known during all my years on my journey with the Lord. I faced temptations I had never faced. As I had begun the process of sanctifying myself for the answer to my desperate prayer, I recognized Satan as he began to show up in my car and in my home, and in my church.

I have Sirius XM on my car radio. I have several stations set for fast access. The station I listen to the most is Enlighten; a southern gospel station. I also have a couple of country music stations set for access. I had made a covenant with the Lord for setting myself aside for the task at hand. This would involve a commitment to **2 Corinthians 6:17, "Wherefore come out from among them, and be ye separate, saith the Lord, and touch not the unclean thing; and I will receive you."** I realized I couldn't listen to anything other than songs that would lift my Spirit and keep my mind on the Lord.

At times when I was in the car by myself, Satan would tempt me to hit the Willie's Roadhouse button, or the classic country button, and I would have to resist that temptation. I would be tempted to make negative comments on Facebook. So, I took myself off Facebook for my season of testing.

Every day, I would face another temptation of things that had never before bothered me. I knew that I had made a covenant with my Lord, and I was not going to allow Satan to interfere and cause me to be defeated. If the enemy could get by me in my time of intercession for my Grandson, victory would never come for him. I knew I could shake off the defeat and blame my defeat on other things or other people, and even God Himself. I also knew this had gotten to the desperate state in my Grandson's life.

I would tell him, "God's got this. You're going to get the job you've applied for." His reply would be, "Yea right, Papaw, God doesn't owe me anything. He's not concerned about my problem; I'm just waiting on another rejection letter." He knew if he got the job it would have to be a God thing, and he felt that his past had voided any favor with God.

This is why there are times when a stronger person in the family has to step up and stand in the gap. That became my place. I made up my mind that if Jesus Christ, the Son of God could stand in the gap for me and die in my place, the least I could do was sacrifice for my grandson.

Even my wife would say little things like, "Maybe he needs to look into some other options, maybe police work isn't what he should be doing. It doesn't look like they're going to call him."

Others would come along with negative words and try to place negative thought in my mind. At these times, I had to tell them not to mess with my faith. God had this and he was going to get the job he had applied for.

It's not easy to spend weeks and months separating yourself in prayer and fasting for something like this. Then, there are the blessed times when God sends a special song, a special message, a special word of encouragement. There are those times when I seem to hear my Heavenly Father say, "You are doing good. Keep walking in the path I have you on. Stay strong. I am with you. I have this. It's going to be okay."

I watched my grandson grow in his faith, and heard him making statements of encouragement, as he was getting closer to the Lord in his walk with Him. He had to get to the place where he knew that when he got the job on this police force, it would have to be God and nothing or anyone else. It would be a certified miracle of God.

The answer to this desperate situation didn't come over night, it took several months--background checks, reference checks, physical testing, an endless list of things that took a lot of time. As I sit here at my desk, feeling the strength of my Heavenly Father, my grandson is at his post of duty, on his new job with a truly great Police Department, with commendations and accolades in other departments, and with his commendations as a great K-9 Officer for six years on another department. All this blessing, after two resignations from two other departments, after mounds of rejection letters from every place he had applied, wanting someone to at least give him a chance. Now, by the grace of Almighty God; when all hope was gone; when he thought his career was over; God showed up in a mighty way. This didn't happen because of me, or because of any effort on my part. All the glory goes to God. I simply supplied a willing vessel to be used of God.

If you need an answer in a desperate situation, be willing to do your part. Be willing to set yourself aside to be used of the Lord. Be willing to do whatever is necessary. Fast. Pray. Sanctify yourself for the task ahead of you.

It will not be easy. You will need to have the strength of God. You will need to be close enough to God that you can feel the encamping angels of the Lord around you to protect you from the onslaught of Satan. You will be in the fight of your life, but through the sufficient grace of Almighty God you can do this.

You will have times of great sorrow, when you hear the enemy tell you that your work is in vain, that you are doing a foolish thing, and that you will be laughed at when it doesn't come to pass. You will have times when those closest to you will say well-meaning words that discourage. You will have spiritual highs and spiritual lows, until you feel like you are on a roller-coaster ride.

You must make up your mind that your praying is not in vain, and you must make up your mind that you will stand against all the wiles of the enemy. These are times you will have to live and pray, Romans 2:7, Galatians 6:9, 2 Thessalonians 3:13, 1 Peter 2:15, 1 Peter 3:17, and 1 Peter 4:19.

Romans 2:7 To them who by patient continuance in well doing seek for glory and honour and immortality, eternal life:

Galatians 6:9 And let us not be weary in

well doing: for in due season we shall reap, if we faint not.

2 Thessalonians 3:13 But ye, brethren, be not weary in well doing.

1 Peter 2:15 For so is the will of God, that with well doing ye may put to silence the ignorance of foolish men:

1 Peter 3:17 For it is better, if the will of God be so, that ye suffer for well doing, than for evil doing.

1 Peter 4:19 Wherefore let them that suffer according to the will of God commit the keeping of their souls to him in well doing, as unto a faithful Creator.

5

Praying The Word

Y̲ou cannot simply read the Word of God. You must also pray the Word of God. Pray the word of God out loud, so the enemy can hear and know that you will not give up or give in. Let him know that you will stand in strong faith and in the amazing grace of Almighty God.

This also lets God know that you mean business. When you pray the Word of God you are drawing close to God and He will draw close to you, and you can resist the devil and he will flee from you. This is what Jesus used against the devil in his time of temptation in the wilderness. The Word tells us that when the devil left Jesus alone, the angels of the Lord came and ministered to Him. They will do the same for you, as you defeat the devil on your journey.

You defeat Satan in your prayer life, not by commitment, but by becoming God's servant. Making a commitment is usually taken very lightly by believers.

On the other hand, a servant belongs to the Master and is totally under His bidding. The only way a Servant can get out from under the ways of the Master is to escape from His control. When a Servant of God walks away from the protecting hand of God, they walk out into a very dangerous place.

I believe that, when a believer walks away from God, that they walk into the control of Satan. There are only two forces at work in the spiritual realm; the force of Almighty God, and the force of Satan. You can not serve them both at the same time.

A servant of God has all the forces of Heaven standing with them in times of battle. The devil leaves you to fight for yourself and will laugh at your defeat.

If you want an effective prayer life, especially in your desperate times, become a true servant of God. Sanctify your life. Lay aside every weight and the sin which so easily hinders you in your praying, and surrender yourself into the hands of a powerful God, Jehovah.

If you have anything against anyone, you cannot expect anything from God. God cannot forgive you, if you cannot forgive others. If you have unforgiveness in your heart, God will not answer your prayers. You must make things right with your fellow man before God will honor you in your prayer life.

Jesus addressed this in the Lord's Prayer.

> **Matthew 6:9 After this manner therefore pray ye: Our Father which art in heaven, Hallowed be thy name.**
>
> **10 Thy kingdom come. Thy will be done in earth, as it is in heaven.**
>
> **11 Give us this day our daily bread.**
>
> **12 And forgive us our debts, as we forgive our debtors.**
>
> **13 And lead us not into temptation, but deliver us from evil: For thine is the kingdom, and the power, and the glory, for ever. Amen.**
>
> **14 For if ye forgive men their trespasses, your heavenly Father will also forgive you:**
>
> **15 But if ye forgive not men their trespasses, neither will your Father forgive your trespasses.**

God forgives us as we forgive others. He holds us accountable for our unforgiveness.

6

Desperately Surrendered

As children of Jehovah, we must realize and know there are some things we face in life that only God can fix. Only God has the answer to what doctors may call, "incurable" or those things we can't fix on our own.

These times are called desperate times. We all face these times on our journey called life. In these desperate times, we call out to God not realizing there are things we must first do in order to touch the throne room of God. In desperate battles, when we can see no way out, we must surrender in order to live through the fight. Surrender in the Christian realm is to sanctify yourself totally to God.

Surrender is not commitment. Surrender means that you are no longer in control. Commitment allows you to still have control.

Good people walk away from well-meaning commitments every day. You cannot say to yourself, "Okay, I will sanctify myself totally to God, then when my desperate prayer is answered, I will go back and live as I was before." No, this is not how you receive anything from a Mighty God.

This surrender is a life changing experience. It is a "Go and sin no more" experience.

Your sin and slack prayer life are what got you in a desperate situation in the first place. You must become a Servant of God, totally surrendered to His will.

When Jesus healed the lame man in John 5, He told the man in verse 5, **"Behold, thou art made whole: sin no more, lest a worse thing come unto thee."** Most of the time, it is not necessarily sin that gets a child of God in trouble. It is that we sometimes forget where God found us, and where He brought us from, to get us to where we are at the present time.

When I first repented of my sins, I was completely changed. I joined the church and trusted God as I would trust a faithful Father. I didn't make a lot of money and could barely make ends meet. Right out of the Navy with a wife and a child, with another one on the way. All I had was a simple child-like faith.

On the way home from church one Sunday morning, I had taken one of our older ladies of the church to her home, and as I was backing out of her driveway, the old car lunged and my baby son was thrown out of the seat into an old guitar. I looked and blood was gushing out of his eyebrow with every beat of his heart. I hurried, not to the emergency room, but back to the church. Pulling up to the parsonage, I knocked on the door. The pastor came out and asked me what was wrong. As I told him, he simply opened the car door and laid his hand on my son and prayed. The bleeding immediately stopped. The pastor went back to finish his dinner and we went home. We were back at church on Sunday night and never had another problem with the cut on his brow.

I learned to place my trust on my Heavenly Father, and He has never failed me. However, over the years, things somehow changed.

As I grew in my faith, accepted the call to preach, and even became lead pastor of a great church, I seemed to become more self-reliant. I found that my Father has a way to get our attention. It seemed that the enemy had launched an all-out attack against my entire family.

My son, who is now grown with children and grandchildren of his own, is the lead pastor of a great church as well. My daughter is a credentialed minister and serves as the Minister of Music at the church where I pastor.

Sickness began to disrupt all of our lives during this attack. We called a family meeting to deal with the enemy. We all knew where the fight was coming from, and we knew that God was our hope and our deliverer.

One of my favorite scriptures is found in **Proverbs 18:10 "The name of the LORD is a strong tower: the righteous runneth into it, and is safe."** This word safe in the Hebrew language is *Sagab*, and means "lofty, strong, set on a high or lofty place, set up on high, to be strong."

This is my powerful promise that came from my Heavenly Father. I have learned over the years, that if I will do my part--if I will surrender myself to God's will for my life as His child--then, all the promises of God are mine for the asking. God will not withhold any good thing from his obedient children who will sanctify themselves to Him. When the enemy of my soul comes in like a flood, my God will raise up a standard against him. When I am at my weakest point in life, God is at His best.

You need to understand, when you totally surrender yourself to God, the enemy of your soul will launch an all -out attack against you. When the battle begins to rage, remember Psalm 37:9, Psalm 123:2, Isaiah 40:31.

> **Psalm 37:9 For evildoers shall be cut off: but those that wait upon the LORD, they shall inherit the earth.**

Psalm 123:2 Behold, as the eyes of servants look unto the hand of their masters, and as the eyes of a maiden unto the hand of her mistress; so our eyes wait upon the LORD our God, until that he have mercy upon us.

Isaiah 40:31 But they that wait upon the

LORD shall renew their strength; they shall mount up with wings as eagles; they shall run, and not be weary; and they shall walk, and not faint.

Find your strength in the Word of God. Live by the Word. Be victorious by the Word. The answer to every problem can be found in searching the word.

7

A Servant's Prayer

God, through the prophet Jeremiah, tells how we can get to Him.

Jeremiah 29:13, And ye shall seek me, and find me, when ye shall search for me with all your heart.

Several places in the Bible tell us that that we are to love the Lord our God with all our heart and with all our soul. If you cannot do this, do not expect any favor from God.

It's like the year of jubilee in Leviticus. If a man was poor and owed money to another man and could not pay the debt, the debtor was to be taken as a servant to the other person. He could not be taken as a bondservant, which was one who was placed in bondage as a slave or one who was made to serve in any capacity. But, he was to serve as a hired servant, which was a person in temporary service who was to work for wages, either by the day or the year. When the trumpet sounded at the year of jubilee, he would be set free to go home to his family, free from debt.

We are the servants of God. As such, we are to work for him until the sound of the trumpet. We will then be free to go to our heavenly home, free from any debt, because Jesus paid our debt at Calvary.

When we develop a true servant-of-God mentality, and we are desiring to please Him, we will find favor with God. You will need the favor of God in order to get answers to your desperate prayers.

Desperate need is much different from daily need. We all have daily needs. Some things we face daily, such as going to work, taking care of the family, and taking care of the home. These things we take care of daily, and God helps us with these needs.

However, there are those times when we face those things that we can't take care of on our own. There are times when the Doctor says we have some terrible thing wrong with us; those times when our employer tells us we are no longer needed; those times when things come into our lives that become dark tunnels with no end and with no way out. Those are the times when only God can bring us through with victory. Those truly are desperate times. These are the times when we must examine ourselves and seek after the favor of God. We must be willing to do whatever it takes to make it. When all you have is God. God is all you need.

Desperate times call for desperate prayer. Desperate praying requires desperate, life-changing living, allowing God in you to become greater than your desperate problem.

Psalm 112:1 Praise ye the LORD. Blessed is the man that feareth the LORD, that delighteth greatly in his commandments.

2 His seed shall be mighty upon earth: the generation of the upright shall be blessed.

3 Wealth and riches shall be in his house: and his righteousness endureth for ever.

4 Unto the upright there ariseth light in the darkness: he is gracious, and full of compassion, and righteous.

5 A good man showeth favour, and lendeth: he will guide his affairs with discretion.

6 Surely he shall not be moved for ever: the righteous shall be in everlasting remembrance.

7 He shall not be afraid of evil tidings: his heart is fixed, trusting in the LORD.

8 His heart is established, he shall not be afraid, until he see his desire upon his enemies.

9 He hath dispersed, he hath given to the poor; his righteousness endureth for ever; his horn shall be exalted with honour.

10 The wicked shall see it, and be grieved; he shall gnash with his teeth, and melt away: the desire of the wicked shall perish.

8

Sacrificially Praying

What does it take, in the life of a child of God, for us to receive what we need from our Heavenly Father? Romans 12:1-2 gives us the answer. We're to live our lives as a Living Sacrifice unto the Lord.

> **Romans 12:1 I beseech you therefore, brethren, by the mercies of God, that ye present your bodies a living sacrifice, holy, acceptable unto God, which is your reasonable service.**
>
> **2 And be not conformed to this world: but be ye transformed by the renewing of your mind, that ye may prove what is**

that good, and acceptable, and perfect, will of God.

I have studied and preached on this, but I have never fully understood it, until I look at it from the Apostle Paul's perspective. Paul saw things as the orthodox Jews saw them. He explained things in the context of Old Testament law, in order for the Jews to understand Christianity.

Paul said to the Roman Christian Jews, "I beseech you therefore, brethren, by the mercies of God, that ye present your bodies a living sacrifice, holy, acceptable unto God, which is your reasonable service." You will need to go back to the Old Testament law of sacrifice In order to understand what Paul is implying.

Their sacrifice system included several types of offerings. There were:

1- *Expiatory Offerings*, which included sin offerings, guilt offerings, and efficacy offerings.

2- *Consecretory Offerings*, which would include burnt offerings, cereal offerings, and drink offerings, (or libation offerings.)

3- *Communal Offerings*, which included peace offerings, thank offerings, votive offerings, free-will offerings, and ordination offerings.

In order to understand what it takes to get our desperate prayers answered, we need to look mainly at the sin offering. The Sin Offering is found 118 times in

107 verses in the Old Testament. It is not found in the New Testament.

The animal brought for the sin sacrifice had to be suited to the rank of the person who was offering it. The High Priest was to bring a young bull, as did the congregation, except where a ritual infraction was involved.

> **Numbers 15:24 "Then it shall be, if ought be committed by ignorance without the knowledge of the congregation, that all the congregation shall offer one young bullock for a burnt offering, for a sweet savour unto the LORD, with his meat offering, and his drink offering, according to the manner, and one kid of the goats for a sin offering.**
>
> **25 And the priest shall make an atonement for all the congregation of the children of Israel, and it shall be forgiven them; for it is ignorance: and they shall bring their offering, a sacrifice made by fire unto the LORD, and their sin offering before the LORD, for their ignorance.**

A Ruler was to bring a male goat. The common person could bring a female goat, or they could bring a lamb. A poor person could bring two turtledoves, or two young pigeons. One of those pairs could serve as a burnt offering; or in extreme cased he might even substitute a tenth of an ephah of fine flower.

Leviticus 5:4 Or if a soul swear, pronouncing with his lips to do evil, or to do good, whatsoever it be that a man shall pronounce with an oath, and it be hid from him; when he knoweth of it, then he shall be guilty in one of these.

5 And it shall be, when he shall be guilty in one of these things, that he shall confess that he hath sinned in that thing:

6 And he shall bring his trespass offering unto the LORD for his sin which he hath sinned, a female from the flock, a lamb or a kid of the goats, for a sin offering; and the priest shall make an atonement for him concerning his sin.

7 And if he be not able to bring a lamb, then he shall bring for his trespass, which he hath committed, two turtledoves, or two young pigeons, unto the LORD; one for a sin offering, and the other for a burnt offering.

8 And he shall bring them unto the priest, who shall offer that which is for the sin offering first, and wring off his head from his neck, but shall not divide it asunder:

9 And he shall sprinkle of the blood of the sin offering upon the side of the altar; and the rest of the blood shall be wrung out at the bottom of the altar: it is a sin offering.

10 And he shall offer the second for a burnt offering, according to the manner:

and the priest shall make an atonement for him for his sin which he hath sinned, and it shall be forgiven him.

11 But if he be not able to bring two turtledoves, or two young pigeons, then he that sinned shall bring for his offering the tenth part of an ephah of fine flour for a sin offering; he shall put no oil upon it, neither shall he put any frankincense thereon: for it is a sin offering.

The person who brought the offering would present the animal and execute the symbolic act of laying on of hands. Aaron and his sons would place their hands on the head of the animal, which symbolically placed the sin of the person on the animal, then the animal was killed and sacrificed for that person's sins. This ritual had to be carried out throughout the entire Old Testament, for forgiveness of sin.

God knew that man would go right back out, and he would commit sin over and over again, because he had been born with the sinful nature of Adam. There had to be a way to bring man back to God.

Isaiah prophesied of the Lord Jesus Christ.

Isaiah 53:1 Who hath believed our report? and to whom is the arm of the LORD revealed?

2 For he shall grow up before him as a tender plant, and as a root out of a dry ground: he hath no form nor comeliness; and when we shall see him, there is no beauty that we should desire him.

3 He is despised and rejected of men; a man of sorrows, and acquainted with grief: and we hid as it were our faces from him; he was despised, and we esteemed him not.

4 Surely he hath borne our griefs, and carried our sorrows: yet we did esteem him stricken, smitten of God, and afflicted.

5 But he was wounded for our transgressions, he was bruised for our iniquities: the chastisement of our peace was upon him; and with his stripes we are healed.

6 All we like sheep have gone astray; we have turned every one to his own way;

and the LORD hath laid on him the iniquity of us all.

7 He was oppressed, and he was afflicted, yet he opened not his mouth: he is brought as a lamb to the slaughter, and as a sheep before her shearers is dumb, so he openeth not his mouth.

8 He was taken from prison and from judgment: and who shall declare his generation? for he was cut off out of the land of the living: for the transgression of my people was he stricken.

9 And he made his grave with the wicked, and with the rich in his death; because he had done no violence, neither was any deceit in his mouth.

10 Yet it pleased the LORD to bruise him; he hath put him to grief: when thou shalt make his soul an offering for sin, he shall see his seed, he shall prolong his days, and the pleasure of the LORD shall prosper in his hand.

11 He shall see of the travail of his soul, and shall be satisfied: by his knowledge shall my righteous servant justify many; for he shall bear their iniquities.

12 Therefore will I divide him a portion with the great, and he shall divide the spoil with the strong; because he hath poured out his soul unto death: and he was numbered with the transgressors; and he bare the sin of many, and made intercession for the transgressors.

John said of Jesus, in **Revelation 13:8 "And all that dwell upon the earth shall worship him, whose names are not written in the book of life of the Lamb slain from the foundation of the world."**

The plan of God for a perfect lamb to be slain for the sins of man was made possible from the very beginning of time. There had to be a way made for this sacrifice. It had to be a lamb without spot or blemish. There must be a lamb without sin, no flaws, no mistakes, no evil.

Hebrews 4:14 Seeing then that we have a great high priest, that is passed into the heavens, Jesus the Son of God, let us hold fast our profession.

15 For we have not an high priest which cannot be touched with the feeling of our infirmities; but was in all points tempted like as we are, yet without sin.

16 Let us therefore come boldly unto the throne of grace, that we may obtain mercy, and find grace to help in time of need.

Then you will need to look at Hebrews 9 for the rest of the story.

> **Hebrews 9:1** Then verily the first covenant had also ordinances of divine service, and a worldly sanctuary.
>
> **2** For there was a tabernacle made; the first, wherein was the candlestick, and the table, and the showbread; which is called the sanctuary.
>
> **3** And after the second veil, the tabernacle which is called the Holiest of all;
>
> **4** Which had the golden censer, and the ark of the covenant overlaid round about with gold, wherein was the golden pot that had manna, and Aaron's rod that budded, and the tables of the covenant;
>
> **5** And over it the cherubims of glory shadowing the mercy seat; of which we cannot now speak particularly.
>
> **6** Now when these things were thus ordained, the priests went always into the first tabernacle, accomplishing the service of God.
>
> **7** But into the second went the high priest alone once every year, not without

blood, which he offered for himself, and for the errors of the people:

8 The Holy Ghost this signifying, that the way into the holiest of all was not yet made manifest, while as the first tabernacle was yet standing:

9 Which was a figure for the time then present, in which were offered both gifts and sacrifices, that could not make him that did the service perfect, as pertaining to the conscience;

10 Which stood only in meats and drinks, and divers washings, and carnal ordinances, imposed on them until the time of reformation.

11 But Christ being come an high priest of good things to come, by a greater and more perfect tabernacle, not made with hands, that is to say, not of this building;

12 Neither by the blood of goats and calves, but by his own blood he entered in once into the holy place, having obtained eternal redemption for us.

13 For if the blood of bulls and of goats, and the ashes of an heifer sprinkling the unclean, sanctifieth to the purifying of the flesh:

14 How much more shall the blood of Christ, who through the eternal Spirit offered himself without spot to God, purge your conscience from dead works to serve the living God?

15 And for this cause he is the mediator of the new testament, that by means of death, for the redemption of the transgressions that were under the first testament, they which are called might receive the promise of eternal inheritance.

16 For where a testament is, there must also of necessity be the death of the testator.

17 For a testament is of force after men are dead: otherwise it is of no strength at all while the testator liveth.

18 Whereupon neither the first testament was dedicated without blood.

19 For when Moses had spoken every precept to all the people according to the law, he took the blood of calves and of goats, with water, and scarlet wool, and hyssop, and sprinkled both the book, and all the people,

20 Saying, This is the blood of the testament which God hath enjoined unto you.

21 Moreover he sprinkled with blood both the tabernacle, and all the vessels of the ministry.

22 And almost all things are by the law purged with blood; and without shedding of blood is no remission.

23 It was therefore necessary that the patterns of things in the heavens should be purified with these; but the heavenly things themselves with better sacrifices than these.

24 For Christ is not entered into the holy places made with hands, which are the figures of the true; but into heaven itself, now to appear in the presence of God for us:

25 Nor yet that he should offer himself often, as the high priest entereth into the holy place every year with blood of others;

26 For then must he often have suffered since the foundation of the world: but now once in the end of the world hath he

appeared to put away sin by the sacrifice of himself.

27 And as it is appointed unto men once to die, but after this the judgment:

28 So Christ was once offered to bear the sins of many; and unto them that look for him shall he appear the second time without sin unto salvation.

Now the plan of God for the perfect lamb is finished. It is laid out for all to see and understand. However, there still must be a sacrifice for sin. We can read and study the word of God, and see that the blood of bulls and goats could not pay the price demanded for our sins.

Hebrews 10:1 For the law having a shadow of good things to come, and not the very image of the things, can never with those sacrifices which they offered year by year continually make the comers thereunto perfect.

2 For then would they not have ceased to be offered? because that the worshippers once purged should have had no more conscience of sins.

3 But in those sacrifices there is a remembrance again made of sins every year.

4 For it is not possible that the blood of bulls and of goats should take away sins.

5 Wherefore when he cometh into the world, he saith, Sacrifice and offering thou wouldest not, but a body hast thou prepared me:

6 In burnt offerings and sacrifices for sin thou hast had no pleasure.

7 Then said I, Lo, I come (in the volume of the book it is written of me,) to do thy will, O God.

8 Above when he said, Sacrifice and offering and burnt offerings and offering for sin thou wouldest not, neither hadst pleasure therein; which are offered by the law;

9 Then said he, Lo, I come to do thy will, O God. He taketh away the first, that he may establish the second.

10 By the which will we are sanctified through the offering of the body of Jesus Christ once for all.

11 And every priest standeth daily ministering and offering oftentimes the same sacrifices, which can never take away sins:

12 But this man, after he had offered one sacrifice for sins for ever, sat down on the right hand of God;

13 From henceforth expecting till his enemies be made his footstool.

14 For by one offering he hath perfected for ever them that are sanctified.

15 Whereof the Holy Ghost also is a witness to us: for after that he had said before,

16 This is the covenant that I will make with them after those days, saith the Lord, I will put my laws into their hearts, and in their minds will I write them;

17 And their sins and iniquities will I remember no more.

18 Now where remission of these is, there is no more offering for sin.

19 Having therefore, brethren, boldness to enter into the holiest by the blood of Jesus,

20 By a new and living way, which he hath consecrated for us, through the veil, that is to say, his flesh;

21 And having an high priest over the house of God;

22 Let us draw near with a true heart in full assurance of faith, having our hearts sprinkled from an evil conscience, and our bodies washed with pure water.

23 Let us hold fast the profession of our faith without wavering; (for he is faithful that promised;)

Notice especially verse 16, **"This is the covenant that I will make with them after those days, saith the Lord, I will put my laws into their hearts, and in their minds will I write them;"** Now, with this verse in mind, look back at **Romans 12:1-2 "I beseech you therefore, brethren, by the mercies of God, that ye present your bodies a living sacrifice, holy, acceptable unto God, which is your reasonable service. And be not conformed to this world: but be ye transformed by the renewing of your mind, that ye may prove what is that good, and acceptable, and perfect, will of God.**

When we come to the saving knowledge of the blood of the Lamb of Almighty God. we come and repent of our sins, then, there has to be a sacrifice. That sacrifice must be the person who is repenting.

In the Old Testament, the sacrifice had to die. In the New Testament, the person who comes to Jesus Christ, Our High Priest, must die to sin and live in Christ.

This is what the Apostle Paul is talking about to the Galatians.

Galatians 2:16 Knowing that a man is not justified by the works of the law, but by the faith of Jesus Christ, even we have believed in Jesus Christ, that we might be justified by the faith of Christ, and not by the works of the law: for by the works of the law shall no flesh be justified.

17 But if, while we seek to be justified by Christ, we ourselves also are found sinners, is therefore Christ the minister of sin? God forbid.

18 For if I build again the things which I destroyed, I make myself a transgressor.

19 For I through the law am dead to the law, that I might live unto God.

20 I am crucified with Christ: nevertheless I live; yet not I, but Christ liveth in me: and the life which I now live in the flesh I live by the faith of the Son of God, who loved me, and gave himself for me.

When an animal was brought to the priest for a sin offering under the Old Testament law, the animal was never going to go back to where or what it was before. It was going to die. It would never be what it was before. It was going to give up its old way of life and would never graze in the fields again.

Now, under the New Testament law, we become a different kind of sacrifice. The word of God tells us that we die out to sin and that the law of God will be in us. We will walk in that law of God every day of our existence on earth. We are then to become a living sacrifice. A sacrifice that is Holy and acceptable in the sight of God and in the sight of others. We literally lay our lives on the line for the cause of Jesus Christ and what He desires of our lives.

If you want an answer to prayer in your desperate times, be a living sacrifice. Be holy and acceptable to God at all times. God has a way, and His way is never our way.

An animal of sacrifice was totally yielded to the law of God. They gave their lives for the sins of others, even though they had no part in the sins. Jesus died for our sin to be forgiven, even though He had no part in our sins. Jesus became our sacrifice.

If you want to develop an effective prayer life, you must first be willing to become a living sacrifice. Paul says this is your "reasonable service." It is the least you can do. It is the rational, logical thing to do.

Then Paul instructed the church not to be conformed to the world, but to be transformed by the renewing of their minds, that they could prove what is the good and perfect and acceptable will of God. Most people today can't even sacrifice time off their cell phones to eat a meal with their family.

Committing one's self to God is a serious matter. It means serving God in the beauty of holiness and keeping yourself pure from the things of the world. Otherwise, you will never have a successful prayer life.

9

God Will Make A Way

As a young Christian I went through a lot of trials that I didn't understand. I wasn't raised in church, so I had a lot to learn about serving God. In the 1960's I came home from serving in the Navy and had to learn how to live as a civilian all over again.

I had a wonderful wife and a baby boy. I was responsible for providing a living for my family. In a short span of time, we were blessed with a beautiful baby daughter, adding more responsibility. I had a job that paid very little, so I had to find a second job to help with my responsibility of raising a family, while learning how to be a civilian.

Carol and I were living with her parents who were pastoring a church. Her parents moved into the church parsonage leaving us to live in Carol's parents' home. As a young Christian, working two jobs, with a wife and two small children, I had a lot to learn about church and serving God.

My pastor, Rev. James Hamblin was a great help and encouragement. He was a guitarist and actually used that to entice me to come to church, as I play guitar myself. Trust has always been a struggle with me, as I grew up in a large family in the mountains of North Carolina, being ridiculed at school because our family had less than many other people we knew. I had to learn to trust God and His word the hard way in so many areas of life. I am very thankful for God's patience and teaching.

After Carol's Dad and Mom moved out, leaving us to live as a family in their home, a different struggle began. Winters were harsh, money was tight, tempers began to flare. Because of our financial condition and my wife's natural Cherokee beauty, I became extremely jealous, which caused problems in our marriage at times.

Working two jobs and trying my best to survive, we could hardly make ends meet. Things seemed to get worse and worse. Our children would wake up in the night screaming in fear. There was never a peaceful moment even during the daytime. The payment on the house was only a mere $35.00 per month and I struggled to pay that.

There were times, during this season of my life, when I would have to walk to a small country store and buy five gallons of kerosene on credit, walk back to the house, and pour it into a 275 gallon tank just to survive a couple of cold nights. There didn't seem to be any light at the end of my tunnel.

I was at work one day feeling very sorry for myself and was sick of our situation. When break time came, I couldn't even afford to take a break with the other workers. I sat down on a shop flat and began to get angry with God.

I told God, "I do the best I can. I go to church every time the doors are open. I give in offerings. I pledge and pay money toward church projects." Then I got serious as I told Jehovah God, "I pay my tithes every time I get paid, and You said in Malachi 3:10, If I would pay my tithe, you would open the windows of Heaven and pour me out a blessing that I would not have room to receive it. God, it's there, in your word, and I'm not getting it."

I believe there are times when God tests us to see if we will get serious about His word and accept the promises that He places there for us. From that day forward, God began a blessing process that has not ended to this day.

Today my wife and I pastor one of our denomination's top ten churches, in our state. God has blessed us in so many ways.

However, before I explain how God brought us out

of our situation, I want to share an experience I had, that may cause some who read this to think I have lost my mind. I was tested while serving in the Navy and was told that I have an above average IQ. Over the years I have had the privilege of going to college for several years while working in ministry. I have two earned doctorates. So, I am not an ignorant person. Trust me, I have not lost my mind when I share this.

While living in my father-in-law's house, I wouldn't go to sleep at night without a gun within reach. My wife and children lived in fear.

Carol met me at the door one day after work, to tell me there was something wrong with the hot water. Nothing was coming out of the spigot but steam. I called a plumber friend who lived up the road from us and told him the problem. I asked if he could take a look at it. He told me to get my family out of the house, that he was on his way. He came, checked out the water heater and informed me that absolutely nothing was wrong with it. He also informed me that in a few minutes it would have exploded, and would have flattened the house, which was made of blocks.

The devil attempted several times to destroy us in that house. After the conversation with my Heavenly Father I mentioned earlier, things began to take a turn for the better.

There was not a way to lock the front door from the outside of this house. It had to be locked from the inside by a dead-bolt, as well as an old slide lock. We parked in the back of the house and would exit through the back door, which could be locked with a key.

One evening, we were getting ready to go to church for midweek service. I locked the front door and we exited through the back door and got into the car to leave. I had left my Bible in the bedroom, which was in the front of the house. So, I had to go back unto the house to retrieve it. As I started to place the key into the lock, God stopped me. God had never spoken to me before, so it was a strange feeling.

I want to explain something here before I continue. As you would open the back door, you would enter into what was once a back porch that Carol's Dad had closed in as a small bedroom for two of his younger sons. You would then go to the right into the kitchen.

God told me, right there, that He was going to show me the problem, and that He was going to deliver my family from it. He told me not to be afraid, not to look at what he was going to show be, and not to worry about coming home that night.

I placed the key into the lock, opened the door, went into the small room, where there were some of Carol's parents' possessions in boxes to my left. As I started into the kitchen, I felt a presence behind me. Glancing carefully over my shoulder, I saw a thing that was like around four feet tall. It was a green color and looked like a dragon, with strong legs and small arms and a human face with a demonic grin. The house was like a strange swamp with fog and a spider web effect. It was like something from a horror movie. God let me know that this was a demon of fear which had possessed this house for years.

The demon followed me through the kitchen, through the living room, and into the bedroom. I picked up my Bible to leave and it followed me through each room as I left the house. I returned to the car and had to sit there for several minutes before I could start the car and leave. Several days passed before I was able to share this with Carol for fear she would think I had lost my mind.

When we returned home from church, we opened the back door and entered the house. As we entered the living room, the front door which had to be unlocked from the inside was standing open. The demon wanted me to know he was still there and had power to still bring fear to my family. He didn't realize that I had been with my Heavenly Father, and had assurance that my family was going to somehow be delivered from all this.

The very next week, I received a phone call from my older brother who was a car dealer with a lot of contacts. He asked me if I wanted to purchase a home.

My response was, "I would love to own my own home, but I can't afford the $35.00 I'm paying here."

God was about to use my brother, who was a sinner at the time, to keep the promise of God to deliver my family from what He was going to show me.

When God is in it, He will not give up on delivering the promise. When you get serious with God, He gets serious with you.

My brother told me I could afford this home and he was coming to get me to take me to see the house. In a few minutes, he came to pick me up. We drove to the house, which was a beautiful three bedroom home on two acres of land with plenty of room to raise a family. My response again was, "I could never afford anything like this." I was forgetting God's promise of deliverance.

Always remember, God sees you in your desperate situation, and He hears your desperate prayer. But, He waits for you to do desperate commitment in order to receive your promise.

There was a man my brother knew, who was separated from his wife. They had always had marital problems and had a house together for which they owed very little. The man wanted out of the loan and the only way this could happen was to sell the house for what was owed on it. My big brother, being used of God, told me I had to take care of this on that day, within the next couple of hours or the opportunity would be gone. He told me that all I had to do was give the man a thousand dollars and pay the payments of $75.00 per month. That's a little more than twice what I already had trouble paying each month. So, I told my brother, who is being used of God, I don't have a thousand dollars to my name, and I can't afford $75.00 per month. My brother, being used of God said, "I'm going to give you the thousand dollars, and you CAN pay the payments."

I learned that day, if God says it, you can take it to the bank. It will happen. We signed the papers that day, and began to move into our own home, where we raised both of our children without fear.

To let you know what a true miracle of God this was, I was moved to a better position on my job, and received a raise for five consecutive months. We only paid eight thousand dollars for our new home, and God's blessings are still flowing in our lives.

Now, the rest of this story. After Carol and I moved out of our Father-in-law's house, he sold it. The man who bought the house painted it the same color of green as the demon God showed me in the house. A young couple rented the house and moved in with small children. Shortly after moving in, the husband killed his wife in the house. The next couple to move in had problems, and a neighbor watched the man run into the back yard and kill himself with a .357 magnum pistol. The house has since been torn down and nothing stands in its place.

I learned, through this, that Satan can possess your surroundings, but he can never possess a child of God. Since the day God delivered my family from that terrible situation, I have never doubted His delivering power. Nothing is impossible with God.

If you are going through a desperate time in your

life, get desperate with God. Pray desperate prayers, pray sincere prayers. Nothing will get God's attention more than the sincere cries of His children when they are in despair. Simple little flippant prayers will not work. Desperate times call for desperate people to pray desperate prayers.

10

The Old Faith

When we get to the end of ourselves, and our own ability, God can then do His best work in our lives. In order to receive anything from God, there must be a strong faith, and a strong prayer life involved. There must be a willingness to do things God's way, and the church of today seems to have forgotten that. God requires total commitment.

I remember when I first became a Christian in the early 1960's, people in the church had a special kind of faith. When they prayed, they believed that God was going to send an answer to their prayer. They lived in such a way that they could get God's attention. They believed in serving God in the beauty of Holiness, as the bible teaches.

I find that people in the church of today have a different kind of faith. The old faith saw miracles because it was a trusting and believing kind of faith. Today's faith is more of a hope-so kind of faith. I want to take a look at what I believe is a major problem in the church of today.

The word "faith" is only found two places in the Old Testament.

Deuteronomy 32:20, And he said, I will hide my face from them, I will see what their end shall be: for they are a very froward generation, children in whom is no faith

and

Habakkuk 2:4, Behold, his soul which is lifted up is not upright in him: but the just shall live by his faith.

This is the old faith.

Faith spoken of in Deuteronomy is the Hebrew word "*Ay-moon*," which literally means truth, faithfulness, established, trustworthy. It is literally talking about God's people who have none of this, and God is displeased with them. He told them that He would hide His face from them.

The Hebrew word used for faith In Habakkuk, is "*Em-oo-naw*," and means established, firmness, security, fidelity, stability, truthful, steady, faithfulness. The just shall live by his integrity. There was a time when you could trust a man's word.

In the Old Testament, righteous people simply placed their full trust in Jehovah God. They had no set doctrine, just trust and obedience. Honesty and integrity were important.

Habakkuk said a man shall live by his faith. The New Testament says a man shall live by faith.

Jesus has come to earth where He preached, died on an old rugged cross, and rose again with victory. Now faith in the Greek is *"Pis-tis,"* meaning, persuasion, credence, moral conviction, religious truth, truthfulness, reliance upon Jesus Christ, truth, assurance, belief, fidelity, trust in God. Faith now is simply believing that God will do what He said He would do. Now faith, for the child of God, is expressed through Hebrews 11.

> **Hebrews 11:1 Now faith is the substance of things hoped for, the evidence of things not seen.**
>
> **2 For by it the elders obtained a good report.**

Faith is the *"Hoop-os-tas-is,"* of things hoped for. Meaning, the setting under, the essence, the assurance, the confidence of things hoped for.

Then, faith is the *"El-eng-khos"* of things not seen. That means the conviction, the proof, the evidence, the admonishment, the affirmation of things not seen. This is the old faith.

Christians now overcome by the word of their testimony. James teaches us, in **James 1:6-8 "But let him ask in faith, nothing wavering. For he that wavereth is like a wave of the sea driven with the wind and tossed.**

For let not that man think that he shall receive any thing of the Lord. A double minded man is unstable in all his ways."

With all this you would think the disciples were loaded with great faith. They walked daily with Jesus Christ Himself. They were there when Jesus fed the five thousand with a little boy's lunch. They were there when he raised Lazarus from the dead. They were right there when Jesus healed blind Bartimaeus. They were there when Jesus healed the man by the pool, who had been sick for thirty-eight years. They were there when He raised Jairus' daughter from the dead and healed the woman with the issue of blood who had spent everything she had on doctors and bad advice and religious customs. They had seen miracle after miracle and yet, the Lord instruct them constantly about faith.

Jesus instructed them in **Luke 17:6, And the Lord said, If ye had faith as a grain of mustard seed, ye might say unto this sycamine tree, Be thou plucked up by the root, and be thou planted in the sea; and it should obey you.** Then, again in **Matthew 21:21-22**, after placing a curse on a fig tree for not bearing fruit, and the disciples were amazed that it withered so quickly, "**Jesus answered and said unto them, Verily I say unto you, If ye have faith, and doubt not, ye shall not only do this which is done to the fig tree, but also if ye shall say unto this mountain, Be thou removed, and be thou cast into the sea; it shall be done. And all things, whatsoever ye shall ask in prayer, believing, ye shall receive.**

The disciples of Jesus had great instruction, and great examples from the greatest teacher who ever lived; but Jesus was constantly rebuking them for their lack of faith. They just couldn't seem to get it right.

I have known people in my lifetime who were people of old faith--people who never allowed their faith to waver. These people did business in the heavenlies.

The devil must have shouted for joy when my godly Mother, Clarice King, went home to be with the Lord. He must have had a celebratory party when old Sister Edna Allred from the Thomasville Church of God went home. She would not give up when she made up her mind that I was going to get saved and join the church. She prayed for me every day. The devil must have really had a running fit when R. W. Shores breathed his last breath that day sitting in an old rocking chair, and went into the presence of God before the rocker stopped rocking. The devil probably breathed a sigh of relief when my wife's mother, Bernice Shores left this earth for her Heavenly home. This was a woman who went during a drought and prayed for rain on her little garden that her and her retired husband needed, and a shower came in just that spot, and her garden produced vegetables all summer that year.

The early church had old, biblical faith. It was that old faith that brought many people through the great depression in 1929 through 1939; which began after the stock market crashed sending wall street into a panic and wiped out millions of investors. Many millionaire investors jumped out of tall buildings ending their lives. Christians suffered as well, but they placed their trust in God to bring them through, and He did, because of their unwavering faith.

Old faith is what brought Christian service men and women home from world war two after the great depression. Old faith kept families together. It caused parents to see their children saved. Old faith produced miracles in the church.

Over the years, I have watched as a new faith began to emerge in the church. Pastors began to hunger for a better salary, and a larger congregation to bring glory to man and not to God.

We lost something when the name-it-and-claim it movement began to raise its head in the church. Christians began to trust their own ability more than God. The church became numbers minded and earthly minded, and program minded, and lost its trust in Jehovah God and spiritual matters.

Paul warned young Timothy of a day which would come and now is here.

2 Timothy 4:1 I charge thee therefore before God, and the Lord Jesus Christ, who shall judge the quick and the dead at his appearing and his kingdom;

2 Preach the word; be instant in season, out of season; reprove, rebuke, exhort

with all longsuffering and doctrine.

3 For the time will come when they will not endure sound doctrine; but after their own lusts shall they heap to themselves teachers, having itching ears; 4 And they shall turn away their ears from the truth, and shall be turned unto fables.

Faith in the church of today has become a fable, a fairy tale. It is like something we see, but do not really believe.

When the church had old faith, people were desperate. Most people didn't have a bank account. Families only had one car, and if you wanted to go on a date you would need to ask Dad if you could use it.

Old faith made sinning children miserable. Old faith made sinning co-workers a little nervous. Old faith made chickens lay eggs to feed hungry children. Old faith kept flour in the flour bin when there wasn't enough money to keep putting any in. Old faith kept food on the table when you didn't know where the next meal was coming from. Old faith kept clothes on the family when you didn't know how it was going to happen. Old faith simply trusted in a God who owned the cattle on a thousand hills.

In our modern society, the new faith says, "I hope it can happen. I hope God can heal me. I hope my children will get saved." Children of God must get back to having trust in the Father that He can do what He tells us He will do.

I remind you that Romans 12 tells us what we need to do.

> **Romans 12:1 I beseech you therefore, brethren, by the mercies of God, that ye present your bodies a living sacrifice, holy, acceptable unto God, which is your reasonable service.**
>
> **2 And be not conformed to this world: but be ye transformed by the renewing of your mind, that ye may prove what is that good, and acceptable, and perfect, will of God.**
>
> **3 For I say, through the grace given unto me, to every man that is among you, not to think of himself more highly than he ought to think; but to think soberly,**

according as God hath dealt to every man the measure of faith.

If we live right, and we are willing to sacrifice for the cause of Jesus Christ, and we set ourselves apart from the things of the world--if we are truly desire God's blessings in the good and perfect will of God—then God has given us the measure of faith. That faith can grow, or it can decrease, it is up to us.

We can have old faith, or we can live in the new faith. When we get desperately in need, we are going to need a know-so faith. In desperate times, a hope-so faith will not get anything from God. It is up to us.

If the church of today is to survive these perilous times we must get back to full trust in God. Old faith says, "God said it. I believe. That settles it." New faith doubts that God even cares and it doesn't even know the promises of God. New faith keeps believers from studying the word of God, therefore, they don't even know what has been promised.

11

God Is Faithful

If God never does another thing for me, as long as I live on this earth, I have already seen enough of my prayers answered that I will still believe.

Beginning in 1969, my family began a singing ministry which consisted of my wife and myself, my nine year old son Allen and my seven year old daughter Candy, along with a good friend, Vestle Widener. We were known as the King's-Way Quartet.

We traveled for twelve and a half years and were gaining in popularity. We stayed booked up for two years in advance. We had a three bedroom, custom built tour bus. We were recording and writing songs and doing very well. We were getting to sing with a lot of the top groups of that time.

In 1981, Allen was now married to Regina. Candy was getting married. We were still traveling and singing, when God told Carol and myself to sell the bus and go to Shelby NC, and take a small church as Senior Pastor.

There was a bad recession that year, and jobs were almost impossible to find. I had been an evangelist now for twelve and a half years.

I had never been a pastor before, and I had very little knowledge in that field of ministry. Leaving our home and ministry was an extremely hard thing to do. We were living in a nice brick home and enjoying a great music and evangelistic ministry.

The church we were assigned to only had eight people, had gotten over $3,500.00 behind in church payments, and was about to go into foreclosure. The parsonage was in very bad condition. It was an old mill house that had been given to the church from a road construction site, which had been moved to the church property and set up. There was no heating or air conditioning system. There was no insulation, and no other pastor would live in it. My only hope was my godly companion who was willing to do whatever it took to be in God's will for our lives.

When I mentioned that I may have made a great mistake, she would tell me we were in God's will and everything would be okay.

It was all quite an adjustment. After preaching to thousands, I was now preaching to six to ten people.

I went to the bank, in an attempt to keep our church out of foreclosure. I sat in the president's office and let him know that God and our denomination had sent me to this church, and that with God's help we were going to catch up the church payments and pay the property off. The man got up from his seat behind his desk, looked me in the eye and said, "Preacher, I've heard it before, I hope you can, I don't want to own a church." And he walked out the door. That wasn't what I wanted or expected to hear. I sat there feeling so defeated. Then I looked at a plaque on his wall that said, "What can't destroy me makes me stronger." I took that as my sign from the Lord.

I went to the church and prayed for a very long time, then went to the parsonage and shared the news with Carol, who was still positive that we were in God's hands, and everything would still be okay.

After much desperate prayer, God told me to take a piece of poster board and draw a picture of the church. Then He told me to section it off in different sections and place an amount of money in each section from five dollars to two thousand dollars. Then He told me that Carol and myself were to place our name in the first two thousand dollar sections. We were then to encourage the few church members to do the same, and place their name in a section as a pledge to help pay off the indebtedness of the church.

Remember, we are in a recession. Neither Carol or myself can get a job. Carol has a degree in accounting and still couldn't find work.

When we decided to get serious with God, God got serious with us once again. On a good week my salary at the church may be seventy-five dollars, and our monthly bills were the same as when we made a good living in what we were doing before we took the church as senior pastor.

One Monday morning, Carol and I got up to start our day, and there was not anything in the house to eat. The cabinets were completely empty. I didn't get a payday that week. The church had to come first. We had decided that, if necessary, we would fast that week. Around eight o'clock that morning one of our elder men of the church knocked on the door. He had two paper grocery bags in his arms, so I invited him in. He shared with us that God had awakened him around six that morning and told him to go to the grocery store and get certain items and bring them by the parsonage. In those two bags was a large loaf of bread, a quart of honey, a package of butter, a bag of Folgers Coffee and several cans of soup. That week we had buttered toast and honey with our coffee for breakfast, and soup for our other meals.

One day, after much prayer, I drove into the driveway and checked the mailbox. In the mail was a card from the first couple I married as a minister. They lived in Winston Salem, and both had good jobs. These folks had sent us a check and shared with us that God had woken them up in the middle of the night and instructed them to send that amount of money. Then they said PS, God said for us to send this amount each month until He tells us to stop. That check was the exact amount of money we owed each month. They paid our bills until the church grew to the point that I made a salary that I could pay it myself.

In just a couple of years the church grew. The project that God showed me was complete. We paid off the indebtedness of the church. The bank president and I became friends. I encouraged him and he got back in church as an active member of his home church. I went to the bank to borrow some money to pave the parking lot and paid it off in half the time of the loan.

God began to send people into the church who wanted a place to work and to worship. Carol got a good job where she stayed until we left the church for another pastorate. When our salary reached the place that it would sustain us, the couple sent another card in the mail and told us that when they were praying God told them it was time to stop sending the check, then, PS, we're going to send it two more month for good measure.

I didn't know anything about being a pastor, but it sure felt good when God would show up right on time and take care of us. He always has.

Carol and I stayed at that church for thirteen years. We were then called of God, to go to another place, where we were needed, to bring healing to a church that was broken by a church split. We have presently been the Senior pastor at this church for twenty-five years. We have seen many miraculous things happen here.

With the help and direction of God, we have built a large fellowship building, and a new church in our time here. Our church is totally debt free.

We serve a powerful, mighty God who is able to do abundantly and above anything we are able to ask, because He loves us so much. But our Heavenly Father wants and demands our total commitment to Him. May God richly bless you as you commit yourself to His divine will for your life.

Valdese, North Carolina

www.outflowpublishing.com